*Anyone can love the mountains,*
*but it takes soul to love the prairie.*
— from a sign on the
Comanche National Grassland

# Prairie Thunder

## THE NATURE OF COLORADO'S GREAT PLAINS

Dave Showalter

Foreword by
Richard Manning

Published by
*Skyline Press*
Pueblo, Colorado

# Prairie Thunder

## The Nature of Colorado's Great Plains
by Dave Showalter
Foreword by Richard Manning

**\* \* \***

ISBN: 978-1-888845-76-1
Published by Skyline Press
Post Office Box 371
Pueblo, Colorado 81002
Printed in China

Central Shortgrass Prairie Ecoregion map
courtesy of The Nature Conservancy

Special thanks to Lucille Egli-McIntyre for
the generous use of her family photos

Historic Rocky Mountain Arsenal photograph
on page 64 provided by the Library of Congress,
Prints and Photographs Division,
Historic American Buildings Survey or
Historic American Engineering Record,
Reproduction Number (Ex:"HABS,ILL,16-CHIG,33-2")

**\* \* \***

ON THE COVER: Storm clouds, Yuma County.
FIRST FRONTISPIECE: Blue grama grass and sky, Bohart Ranch.
SECOND FRONTISPIECE: Sunset at Pawnee Buttes.
TITLE PAGE: A pair of burrowing owl chicks.
RIGHT: Brilliant golden cottonwoods contrast with a blue sky
along the shore of Lake Ladora, one of Rocky Mountain
Arsenal NWR's manmade lakes. The lake was denuded of
vegetation throughout the chemical weapons manufacturing
era, and has rebounded to provide important riparian
habitat as well as great fishing.

For Marla ~
The only journey worth taking is with you.

To learn about places to visit and grassland conservation,
please contact these organizations:

Rocky Mountain Arsenal National Wildlife Refuge
www.fws.gov/rockymountainarsenal

Rocky Mountain Arsenal Wildlife Society
www.rmawildlifesociety.org

Audubon COLORADO
www.auduboncolorado.org

The Nature Conservancy
www.nature.org

Comanche National Grassland
www.fs.fed.us/r2/psicc/coma

Pawnee National Grassland
www.fs.fed.us/r2/arnf/

Rocky Mountain Bird Observatory
www.rmbo.org

Plains Conservation Center
www.plainsconservationcenter.org

Playa Lakes Joint Venture
www.pljv.org

Boulder Open Space and Mountain Parks
www.osmp.org

Colorado Wildlife Federation
www.coloradowildlife.org

Defenders of Wildlife
www.defenders.org

Prairie Dog Coalition
www.prairiedogcoalition.org

Greater Prairie Chicken Tours
www.wraychamber.net

Mountain Plover Festival
www.karval.org

High Plains Snow Goose Festival
www.lamarchamber.com

Prairie Birding Tours
www.coloradobirdingtrail.com

# Table of Contents

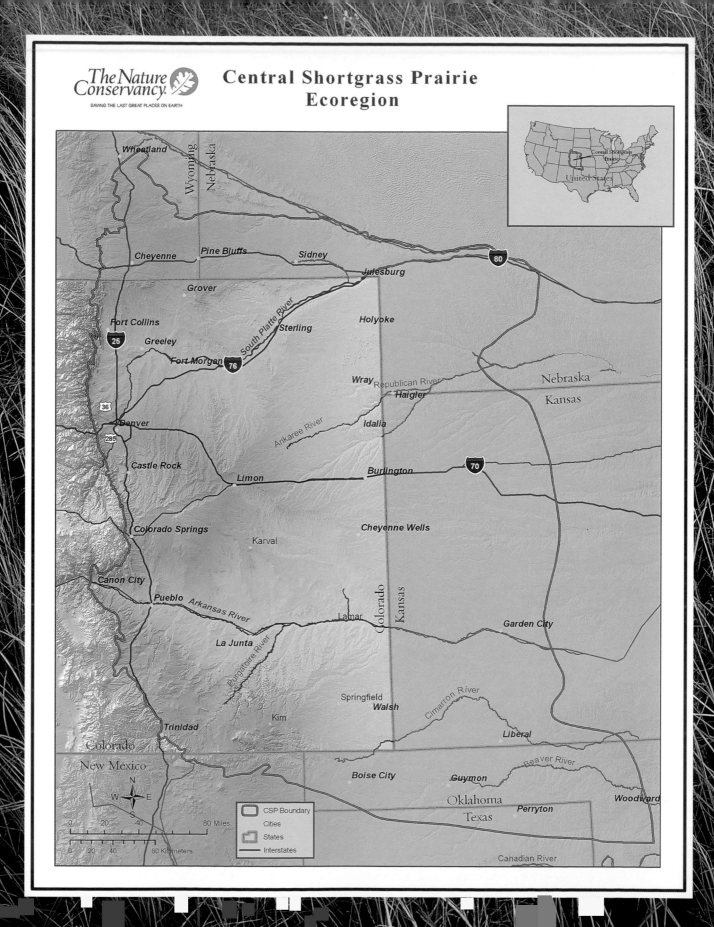

# Foreword ~
# The Promise of Grass
## by Richard Manning

This is not a writer's cheap trick, but true, that literally, as I sat to write this, I was distracted by a gratifying compliment from a whitetail deer. Maybe eight feet outside my study's window, a weeks-old fawn stood and wobbled about my front yard. I'd been at my post a good half hour, but this was the first I'd seen it.

Deadlines be damned, I grabbed a camera and ran to the yard, only to find the fawn had vanished. Then I thought about it and knew better. I hadn't seen a doe, so the fawn would stay put. I searched, finally finding it curled in a tight, spotted ball in wet grass. During the search I had at times been three feet from it, and still had not seen it.

This whole business would be unremarkable enough but for one small fact: my house is urban, a 1950s-issue brick rambler in a long-established neighborhood a half mile from downtown Missoula, Montana. There's a busy street out front and a carpet of neatly clipped bluegrass lawns all around. But not mine.

It is a central tenet of my existence that a lawnmower is an artifact of British colonialism, an anachronistic attachment to English country gardens. Why we persist in planting, mowing and irrigating these biological deserts is a mystery to me. I measure the quality of my life by not owning a lawnmower. I do not mow, I restore.

I bought my house four years ago, ripped out its bluegrass lawn and attendant lollipop trees, over-bred roses, sprinklers and plastic curbing. These plants are to habitat what a Pekinese lap dog is to a wolf. Then, using rootstock and seeds, I brought back a bit of Palouse prairie, the collection of plants native to the valleys of the northern Rockies, my home ground. The matrix—as is the case in all prairies—is grass, bluebunch wheatgrass, Idaho fescue, rough fescue, prairie junegrass. The forbs are yarrow, lupine, blanketflower, bitterroot, and shooting star; the shrubs, sagebrush, rabbitbrush, woods rose, snowberry, a paltry collection by native standards, but a beginning.

This year, the year of the fawn, it finally began to look like the real deal, grasses waste-high and fully flourescent. I suspect some of my neighbors think I am nuts, but not all, given that some of my neighbors are white-tailed deer. The compliment came not from the fawn, but from its mother, which had taken a look at my yard, and said something like "This looks about right," by which she meant, safe, secure enough to stash her fawn for the day. She collected it late that afternoon.

Security. I confess I have come to hate this word as the banner of our chicken-little society. It's odd that I mention security as introduction to a presentation of the stunning visuals of Colorado's short-grass prairie. Yet if you look at prairie long enough, look intently at its many faces, you will find security layered among the multiple meanings. Prairie's wild array of grasses and rolling hills contains a record of our mistakes, arrogance, myths, ideals, hubris, in short, our history. Look at grassland long enough, and strange ideas will pop up as unexpected as a fawn.

Long-earred owls on the nest.

Colorado's grasslands are part of the larger story of prairie, a variation on the theme we think of as uniquely American, as American as cowboys, cattle drives, the Dust Bowl and farm subsidies. Indeed prairie is a central part of the larger American story, in that even easterners and Californians grew up invested in bison, plains Indians and John Wayne.

The biological story that underlies all of this, however, is that we, the European settlers who colonized here, greatly misread the power of the place. The record is clear; it produced wildlife in abundance before whites arrived, but whites then did not regard abundant wildlife as production; farming was production. So we killed the animals and plowed up the grass or grazed it near to death with hordes of exotic cattle. The comeuppance for this was our country's greatest environmental disaster, the Dust Bowl, after which a few of us began reconsidering the terms of habitation of this place. There is still much to learn, but we are now at a turning point.

And by "we," I mean a population much larger than we who are lucky enough to live in and love the grassland American West. The simple fact is, this story is not unique to Colorado, or even the North American plains.

About 6,000 years ago, a culture arose on the banks of the Danube River in what is now eastern Europe. Archaeologists know these people by their distinctive pottery, but the culture is better marked by its agrarian economy based on two species, wheat and beef, a powerful combination that stormed across Europe in a matter of 200 or so years. Fenced in by some transportation issues, the wheat-beef people, aka Caucasians, aka Europeans,

overpopulated the continent, endured plagues and famines, and finally learned how to sail. There are complications and permutations of European colonization, but overall it is dominated by a clear and major theme. The Europeans sought out all of the world's temperate grasslands and exported to them wheat-beef agriculture, lately bolstered by the corn discovered in the New World.

The world's great temperate grasslands besides our grand stretch in North America lie in sub-Siberian Asia, the pampas of South America, Australia, New Zealand and South Africa. All of these places are today dominated by European surnames and wheat-beef-corn agriculture. Put another way, something like 10 percent of all biomes worldwide enjoy some sort of protected status, as parks and reserves. Temperate grasslands are the exception. Only one percent is protected. Agriculture got the rest.

We Europeans have a bedrock bias toward agriculture. We claimed to be civilizing the world, making it democratic, safe and secure, but what we have meant by this is plowing it up, reducing it to bluegrass lawns and wheat fields.

What is challenging us now, though, is that we have gone too far. Certainly we need farming; this is not in contention, but economic pressures of farming pushed plows into ever more arid reaches, to the margins, and the margins have begun to fray. We overplayed our hand, as the Dust Bowl informed, as the depletion of the Ogallala aquifer is about to inform, as $20 billion in annual farm subsidies inform persistently. We can ground truth this in the boarded-up towns of the American plains, now mostly cemeteries and old people, vacant schools, a convenience store and a bar,

Cottonwood trees in fog.

derelict house trailers. The founding assumption of farming was the steady flow of food; that is, farming was to make us secure, but life on the plains feels anything but.

✳ ✳ ✳

My most recent conversation about the security of grassland people was with Samburu tribesmen in villages in the sweeping grasslands surrounding Mount Kenya. The Samburu are cousins of Kenya's more famous Masai, and like them, have lived as nomadic herders for thousands of years. In recent decades, their lives have been precarious, plagued by disease, poverty and the rampant violence that is life in much of Africa. In the last few years, however, their lives have improved somewhat, partly because they have cell phones, partly because they have an income and partly because they have game scouts. The latter two are directly attributable to Ian Craig, the first, indirectly.

Craig is a soft-spoken, polite third-generation Kenyan who began managing his parents' ranch in the late '70s. He was then a hunting guide uninterested in cattle, so he sold his and began restocking the 62,000-acre ranch with wildlife, beginning as a sanctuary for the endangered black rhinoceros. Today it feels like a sanctuary from the drought, green and lush in sharp contrast to the cow-burned over-grazed lands that surround, but the surrounding lands are changing.

About a decade ago, Craig's ranch, now called the Lewa Conservancy, became productive enough to begin spilling wildlife onto Samburu lands. The Samburu regard grassland wildlife much as American ranchers regard prairie dogs and wolves, for analogous reasons, but worse. Elephants, in fact, seek out Samburu cattle and stomp them to death. The Samburu in turn kill elephants with their four-foot-long, poison-tipped spears.

Craig's solution to this conflict was money. He enticed one neighboring Samburu communal ranch into an experiment. The tribe set aside a large area of its ranch for wildlife, welcomed elephants, rhinos and the rest, then, with Craig's help, built a guest lodge for high-end tourists. The lodge produced an income stream that allowed them to build schools and clinics. To prevent poachers, they hired the game scouts who needed a communications network. The scouts stopped poaching, but also patrolled the community, communicated and stopped what was then rampant cattle rustling. They became the eyes and ears of the community, and banditry ceased.

Using this single ranch as an example, Craig signed on seven more communal ranches representing 1.5 million acres of Kenyan grassland now producing wildlife and income. It is tempting to say wildlife built all of this, but Craig will tell you it was grass, and to this day, he is still learning about grass, but he has learned enough to know that properly managed, grassland is far more productive than anyone imagined, including Samburu herders. In fact, his wildlife-grazed grass is now producing some better cattle, the Samburu acknowledge. Meantime, the Samburu cattle are producing better wildlife habitat.

The reason for this is diversity. The collection of grazers and browsers—from the pocket-sized antelope, the dik-dik, to elephants and giraffes—all have different preferences and

Green darner dragonfly.

seasonal needs. Remove a layer of that diversity and the plant community suffers, simply because evolution has used diversity to balance the whole business, what one researcher calls the "great discordant harmony" that is grassland.

Craig's conservancy looks lush and green, but it is in fact, overgrown with some over-ripe grasses. Historically, those grasses have been kept in control by zebras, but zebra numbers have been catastrophically reduced throughout Kenya. The best analogue for zebras is cattle, so Craig invites Samburu herders to enter his wildlife conservancy to help fill the zebra's niche.

I mention all of this because I imagine something very much like it will evolve on the American plains. A decade ago, a coalition of conservation groups surveyed the northern plains from Colorado on north to Saskatchewan and found ten large areas ripe for conservation. Work has already begun in acquiring the biggest and best of these, 3.2 million acres surrounding and including the C.M. Russell Wildlife Refuge in north central Montana. The place now holds prairie dog towns running to thousands of acres and the core of a herd of wild bison. Mule deer, antelope, big horn sheep and elk are all present and poised to proliferate.

So far, this all sounds like a fairly conventional experiment in conservation: set

aside some land, protect it from humanity and human economy, sprinkle in wildlife, then add tourists, a flatlander's Yellowstone. I don't think so.

What's going to happen, whether we intend it or not, is that native grazers and the attendant flora and fauna will restore the discordant harmony, and this stretch of the plains will become more productive than we ever thought. Certainly more productive in the monetary sense; tourism and hunting already bring in more dollars per acre in this area than does ranching. But also more productive on the primary level, more pounds of protein per acre.

Further, I expect some ranchers will figure this out and get smart about inhabiting the plains. They will make money from wildlife, but also realize they are grassmen, not cattlemen, and manage accordingly. And I expect that some conservationists will get smarter about living with ranchers, which is to say, human economy, and that they, like the Africans already are doing, will use cattle when appropriate.

In fact, something very much like this is already occurring with the Malpai Borderlands Group, a coalition of ranchers and conservationists working a grass-banking experiment along the New Mexico-Arizona state line. Significantly, one group in Africa has already

Black-tailed jackrabbit.

arranged an exchange of visits between cowboys from Malpai and Masai herders. I would have given serious money to have seen the Masai rodeo.

What those Masai and cowboys are learning is something far more profound than simply how to grow better grass, that grassland properly realized means the whole is greater than the sum of the parts. Our single-resource, single-use mindset, our slavish devotion to cows and wheat, has greatly reduced the productivity of the plains, but it can be restored. We can bring it back, but we will not bring it back by simply leaving it alone. It will require attention, learning, wisdom, experience, humility.

It will require, above all, seeing. There is a lot more information in the images in this book than you might think, little bits of history and guidance encoded in every view. That's the way grassland works and finally, the real enticement of the place, that its broad craggy face properly read reveals not just its detailed history, but our future. But realizing that future requires that we see grassland for what it is, on its own terms, not as the cherished myths of farmers. Ranchers and conservationists have taught them to see.

Realizing the promise of grass requires that we act. Carefully. Then watch, look for something like a fawn to pop up from the tall grass to testify that we got that little bit of it right. Then think about it, learn, then act again.

Summer skies over Chalk Bluffs.

# Introduction

Standing in a field of gold wildflowers on the Comanche Grassland as morning fog gives way to sun and blue sky, revealing canyon walls and textures of grass and cacti, the aroma of wet sage filling the air—another prairie moment to be captured through the eye of my lens. In these moments, this photo project seems so perfectly natural.

While living in the Denver metro area for more than 20 years, I have always been fascinated by our natural surroundings. All along the Front Range, wildlife sightings are commonplace as we are treated to spectacular sunrises and sunsets, while watching banks of clouds rise from the great Rocky Mountains and drift over the eastern plains. This infatuation with nature close to home was the genesis of this project.

## WHY THE PRAIRIE?

I have grown accustomed to the blank stare when I tell someone that I'm working on a Colorado prairie book, and the inevitable follow up-question, "Why the prairie?" Friends know my wife, Marla and me to be people who love the mountains—climbing fourteeners, backpacking, trekking, the whole bit. I'm also well aware of the common perception that the prairie is flat and boring, a place to drive *through* on the way to the mountains. What happened with me is what happens with a lot of folks; the prairie grew on me. In fact, it burned into my soul. Maybe it's because I took the time to watch and listen, to anticipate the changes within seasons and note the ever-changing nature all around me. That's how it starts. The prairie doesn't have the bowl-you-over scenery of the mountains. It is a subtle beauty that is completely dictated by not only changes of season, but micro changes within seasons. Native grasses may look sparse and over-grazed in March; but visit in August after the monsoon and you may discover an "ocean of grass," waves flowing on the wind. A land that seems devoid of wildlife in the dead of winter comes to life around the first of March; and by May, the abundance of wildlife and rich tapestries

of green can be overwhelming. Missing a few weeks on the prairie requires getting reacquainted—it changes that fast, and something magical happens every day. There is something else, though, a larger emotional connection to grasslands that even the most ardent prairie lovers have trouble articulating. Most just say "I don't know what it is—there's just something about the prairie." In *Grassland,* author Richard Manning discusses human evolution from forest apes, explaining humans' "ability to stand erect and see over the grass, humans fit grassland." Although I love to talk about the emotional reasons to love the prairie, it seems that we evolved with grass and may simply be hard-wired to grassland.

Four years ago, I contacted Rocky Mountain Arsenal National Wildlife Refuge in hopes of further developing my close-to-home photography into a full-blown book project. Timing is everything, and I met with Dean Rundle, then refuge manager at a time when the refuge was in-between photographers. I thought that I knew quite a bit about the Colorado prairie, the arsenal history, the massive mule deer, but I can now readily admit that I didn't know much. I guess I made up for my lack of grassland knowledge with enthusiasm, and Dean gave me the opportunity to become "volunteer photographer" for the arsenal. More than anything else, Dean's trust and this partnership with the U.S. Fish and Wildlife Service (USFWS) is the reason for *Prairie Thunder.* My work at the arsenal is the foundation of this book.

My first interaction with arsenal biologists was photographing a deer study. The Colorado Division of Wildlife (CDOW) partnered with USFWS, trapping does, performing a battery of tests to determine overall health, including field ultrasound, inserting an IUD, and monitoring the deer for two years. The arsenal biologist community welcomed me into their world, answered all of my layman's questions and generally made me feel like a part of their team. My learning has been accelerated by participating in not only the deer study, but small mammal trapping, burrowing owl trapping and banding, bald eagle

Coneflowers.

banding, a bat study, kestrel banding and west Nile testing, bird counting, and visiting the National Black-Footed Ferret Conservation Center. This window into the biological side of prairie preservation has opened my eyes to a level of commitment beyond anything I could have imagined.

My work at Rocky Mountain Arsenal NWR led me to meetings with Gary Graham, PhD., Executive Director of Audubon Colorado. Gary has worked on grassland projects in South America, Texas and Colorado and encouraged me to broaden the scope of the project to include all of eastern Colorado. The shortgrass prairie ecosystem is a top priority for Audubon, largely because prairie birds dominate the Audubon "watch list." These formative discussions led to the structure of *Prairie Thunder*.

The shortgrass prairie ecosystem changed forever with the extirpation of bison and subsequent plow-up of land that should never have been turned over. The land and wildlife are still paying a price for failed land management practices leading up to the dust bowl. With roughly 90% of the central shortgrass prairie privately held, we are learning new ways to manage the land for preservation, while deploying new conservation tools. One of the many surprises on my journey was to learn that land owners and conservationists are not only speaking the same language, but in many cases sharing the same conservation goals.

The Nature Conservancy (TNC) is a leader in grassland conservation and has accelerated their efforts to secure conservation easements from willing sellers and purchase important grassland parcels, which are then leased to experienced local ranchers. TNC helped form the Shortgrass Prairie Partnership, a consortium of private land owners, conservation groups and government agencies to address the wide range of conservation issues facing the central shortgrass prairie. The face of conservation on Colorado's plains is changing at warp speed.

Thanks to partnerships with the Colorado Division of Wildlife, Audubon Colorado, Colorado Field Ornithologists, and the Rocky Mountain Bird

*Clearing fog, cholla and threadleaf flowers in Picture Canyon, Comanche National Grassland.*

Observatory, citizens can visit private ranches and public sites along the Colorado Birding Trail to experience world-class birding and wildlife viewing. We have the opportunity to contribute to uplifting prairie communities with our eco-tourism dollars. Nature is the new currency on the plains.

The project has been a peeling away of layers, erasing many of my pre-conceptions while learning how we arrived at this crossroads. The conservation history is as rich and colorful as the land, while the issues of a century ago affect land management decisions today. Consider that cattle grazing patterns are now managed to mimic bison behavior for the benefit of grassland and wildlife, and you start to get the idea.

*"If you come to a fork in the road, take it."* — *Yogi Berra*

Prairie sunflowers.

My own personal quest has resulted in thousands of photographs, taken from blinds, my truck, a small airplane, windswept plains, canyon and river overlooks, countless sunrises and sunsets (some panned out, some didn't), while covering more than 30,000 miles along the way. The images on these pages were taken with 35mm Nikon equipment, both film and digital, using four different camera bodies and lenses ranging from 18mm to 840mm. With the exception of black-footed ferrets (released into the wild one week later) and some of the bison (by necessity), all of the animals are wild. No "wildlife models" were used. My wife still makes breakfast every time I get up "too early" to go shoot, and applauds the result from each outing. She is a saint. I have sat at numerous kitchen tables on plains ranches, visiting with warm-hearted folks that I just met, with a love of the prairie as my only license for being there.

I am very fortunate that Richard Manning, the foremost author on the North American Great Plains, graced these pages with his foreword. Richard agreed in our first discussion, before seeing any of my work, simply because "it is so important."

A visit to the local bookstore reveals shelves filled with wonderful photography books about Colorado's mountains. There have been relatively few photo books about the Colorado prairie though, and none for two decades. As the concept jelled, it became apparent that the only approach for *Prairie Thunder* was to make a photo conservation book. The imagery reflects my sense of wonder while traveling on a journey to understand the state of conservation on Colorado's shortgrass prairie. To that point, it is a collection of my experiences, not a catalogue of prairie flora, fauna and habitat. The great herds of bison may have vanished, yet much of the land remains intact; and we have the gift of opportunity, a chance to preserve on a grand scale and tell the greatest conservation story ever.

FACING PAGE: Spring storm over a field of ragwort and Mesa de Maya, Las Animas County.

# Prairie Thunder

On a sun-splashed March day, a small crowd anxiously watches the arrival of a tractor-trailer that has been traveling through the night. The cargo is more than eight tons of bison to be transferred from Montana's National Bison Range to Colorado's Rocky Mountain Arsenal National Wildlife Refuge. An anxious buzz is rippling through the group of scouts, Native Americans, dignitaries, refuge employees and local and national media. We are all crouched behind a makeshift fence as instructed, to avoid spooking the animals. The doors are thrown open, and. . .nothing! We had been told they may not want to come out after 15 hours on the road. With Dr. Tom Roffe banging on the trailer, five cows explode from the truck onto the Colorado shortgrass prairie. They are followed by eight more cows; some of them pregnant, and three massive bulls. The bison barely look around, then meander west. Once numbering in the millions and missing from this land for over 100 years, these genetically pure icons of the prairie have finally returned home. The thunder from this release has been heard around the world; sixteen animals symbolize our once wild Great Plains.

# Colorado's Abundant Plain

The great Rocky Mountains slice north to south through Colorado, forming the spine of Colorado's Continental Divide, the southern Rockies. The mountains give way to the foothills and the high plains roll away to the east—a crumpled landscape of big sky over rolling grasslands, buttes, canyons, arroyos, escarpments, rivers and streams. It is neither flat, nor boring. The high plains of Colorado lie on the western reach of the Great Plains in the rain shadow of the Rockies, a semi-arid landscape cut off from moisture flowing from the Pacific. Colorado may be known for its Rocky Mountains, but these high plains make up more than 40 percent of its land mass. Eighty percent of Coloradans live on the shortgrass prairie; it is our home. The Colorado prairie is a patchwork quilt of private and public land that is dry-land farmed, irrigated and grazed. In places where there are buttes, bluffs, canyons and glacial debris, the prairie remains largely undisturbed.

The Great Plains of North America, one of the world's largest ecosystems, is a grassland stretching from Ohio to Colorado, Saskatchewan to Texas. Once called America's Serengeti, they were one of the most abundant ecosystems on Earth. Somewhere between 50 and 70 million bison roamed here, alongside grizzly and black bears, elk, pronghorn, wolves, swift foxes and mountain lions. Prairie dog complexes, or "towns," were 50 or more miles across. A birder's catalogue of avian creatures thrived on the grassland as well, including large numbers and varieties of eagles, hawks, owls, American kestrels, prairie and peregrine falcons, lark buntings (Colorado's state bird) and all manner of songbirds, a dozen species of sparrows, greater and lesser prairie chickens, sage grouse, beaver and dabbling ducks, long-billed curlews, mountain plover, American avocet and more. All thrived here for more than 10,000 years. Part of what intrigued and attracted me to this project is that most of these creatures are still here, despite an increasingly fragmented habitat that has led to declining populations.

Today, less than one percent of North America's shortgrass prairie is protected. It is the least- protected ecosystem on the planet, considered by many to be its most endangered.

It is a land that demands that we leave our cars to hear the song of the meadowlark, or hike to watch a distant butte burn like a match head in the diminishing light of the setting sun. Canyons beg to be explored, offering the gift of discovery, and the weather always promises to be interesting. In some locations, tallgrass grows chest-deep and morning dew will soak your jeans. Some of the greatest avian migrations on Earth take place here, as they have for thousands of years. Those willing to explore and listen will notice a change within that is as hard to describe as the land itself. A passion builds inside anyone who spends time on the prairie. Take a walk, you'll see.

FACING PAGE: Spring green at Pawnee National Grassland.
INSET: Cholla cactus bloom.

The edges of the prairie, where the Great Plains meet the foothills of the Rockies, are ecological hot spots, rich with animal and plant life from both mountains and plains. Prairie falcons and golden eagles nest in pockets of the Flatirons, rock formations in Boulder that were tilted on end when continents collided 300 million years ago. Rising more than 2,000 feet above the plains, these impressive stone slabs are part of the Fountain Formation. The uplift that created the ancestral Rockies formed the Flatirons, as well as the formations at Red Rocks, Roxborough and Garden of the Gods.

Mountains meld into plains at
White Ranch Park, Jefferson County.

Fall colors flank uplifted sandstone fins at
Roxborough State Park, southwest of Denver.

# Prairie Spring

*Each moment of the year has its own beauty. . .*
*a picture which was never before and shall never be seen again.*
—Ralph Waldo Emerson

One day, at the bitter end of a long winter, and whether snow lingers or not, the sweet song of the meadowlark fills the air. It is startling how it seems these birds simply appear overnight. This is the beginning of the spring migration, an annual event that rivals migrations anywhere on the planet. As the bald eagles return to the north, songbirds, dabbling ducks, shorebirds, and raptors rush in to reap the bounty of another prairie spring and summer. By early April, burrowing owls complete their journey from Texas and Mexico, while Swainson's hawks migrate all the way from Argentina and immediately begin their mating and nesting rituals.

The calendar is meaningless in a Colorado spring; March and April are the snowiest months of the year and a blizzard is always a possibility. Animals are driven by an internal clock, though, and every single creature is mating and birthing throughout the spring. Each day brings a new sense of wonder—the chance of finding a newborn fawn in thick, native grass, a tiny sparrow's nest, Swainson's hawks mating high in a cottonwood tree, miniature baby prairie dogs, or a ruddy bison calf roughly nursing.

Wildflowers explode from the prairie soil in May, nurtured by rains and warmer days. A riot of blues, reds, yellows and oranges decorate the verdant grasses. The flowers will last as long as the rain, fading in the late-spring heat. Anytime the prairie is wet, something will bloom —oftentimes flowers not seen in years, patiently lying dormant for perfect conditions.

FACING PAGE: Native needle-and-thread grasses wave in the wind in sharp contrast to the verdant green shale hills on the Comanche National Grassland.
INSET: Male western bluebird perched in a ponderosa pine tree.

The prairie in bloom ~
TOP ROW: Bluebells & Indian paintbrush.
BOTTOM ROW: Blanketflower, yucca pods & wild iris.

FACING PAGE: Arnica carpets ponderosa savannah at Doudy Draw, Boulder Open Space.

INSET: Prickly pear cactus blooms. RIGHT: Flowering yucca below the west butte, Pawnee National Grassland. The Pawnee Buttes and surrounding cliffs are remnants of an ancient seabed.

A river of pink plains penstemon
on The Nature Conservancy's Bohart Ranch.

"Blue Horse," a very well-preserved Plains Indian pictograph drawn after the arrival of Spanish horses 1,400 years ago, Picture Canyon, Comanche National Grassland.

TOP: Western rattlesnake.

BOTTOM: Pedestal rocks in Picketwire Canyon, Comanche National Grassland.

Fresh spring greenery and rock walls in Picture Canyon,
Comanche National Grassland.

A prairie bouquet consisting of blanket flower and western spiderwort.

# Prairie Chickens

Sitting in a blind "too early," as Aldo Leopold called it, gives me time to really listen to the land. One of those times was on private land, outside of Wray, Colorado, in Yuma County. I was sitting in my faded portable hunting blind one April morning, waiting in the dark for greater prairie chickens to arrive. The area where prairie chickens perform their mating display is called a lek, and this particular area is the main lek where most of the activity has gone on for as long as anyone can remember, maybe thousands of years. No one knows why the chickens like this particular spot, except that the ground is pretty bare, which allows prairie chickens to spot predators attracted to the unique "booming" sound of the males. The booming on the lek here in tiny Wray attracts not only female chickens, but birders from all over the world.

The lek is a depression surrounded by sand hills, which are covered by native blue grama grass and yucca. It is a pleasant, rolling landscape. I had heard the booming from a distance from my camp (truck next to a windmill) before sunset and anxiously waited for all hell to break loose in the morning. At 5:00a.m. sharp, even before the meadowlarks started singing, there was an eerie, unnerving sound like plastic trash bags blowing in the wind. I tried to look around, but it was pitch dark, so I sat and wondered what was going on. Moments later, the booming began—like blowing over a pop bottle with an amplifier. I realized the chickens had arrived.

Male greater prairie chickens ~
Mating display (FACING PAGE) and sparring match (ABOVE).

In short order, the sound was deafening, with horned larks and meadowlarks chiming in as the faintest light gave a hint that I was in for quite a show. Greater prairie chickens were everywhere—jumping, strutting and booming, puffing their enormous air sacks in blazing orange to attract a female. They also attracted three coyotes before sunrise, producing a comical attempt for an easy breakfast reminiscent of a coyote and roadrunner cartoon. Before long, the coyotes gave up and the show resumed. In all, there were over 80 birds on the lek, the result of early spring grass fires causing satellite leks to join the main lek. I watched an ancient display for more than three hours and couldn't have asked for better entertainment. I had also witnessed a conservation success story. In the '80s, the greater prairie chicken was state-threatened, a result of grassland habitat converted to cropland. The U.S. Department of Agriculture developed the Conservation Reserve Program (CRP) in cooperation with private landowners to re-establish native prairie. Greater prairie chickens were also reintroduced and are now stable and thriving. Wray has benefitted too, with greater prairie chicken viewing programs creating a strong "chicken tourism economy."

A coyote's unsuccessful attempt to catch breakfast.

LEFT: Wray sandhills.

37

# Bison on the Great Plains

*This scenery already rich pleasing and beautiful
was still further hightened by immense herds of buffaloe,
deer Elk and Antelopes which we saw in every direction
feeding on the hills and plains.*
—Meriwether Lewis, The Journals of Lewis and Clark,
September 17, 1804, in the Dakotas

Recently, I witnessed the miracle of a new bison calf nursing and wondered what it must have been like to stand on a high point and see bison stretching to the horizon in all directions. So many animals, in fact, that a single herd would take *days* to pass. Sixty million bison, each weighing up to a ton, roamed the Great Plains grasslands with grizzlies, wolves and elk for 11,000 years.

Plains Indians lived as nomads tracking bison across the plains. The Colorado Plains Indians were purely a culture based on bison; meat-eating nomads following grass-eating nomads. Early hunting methods weren't at all selective—bison were simply chased en masse over cliffs, or buffalo jumps. Skinning and carving up a few hundred bison involved the whole tribe and must have been both a joyous and strenuous process.

Hunting changed dramatically 1,400 years ago after the arrival of the Spanish horse,

a creature perfectly suited for the American Indian lifestyle. Indian hunters could selectively hunt younger, more tender bison and kill only what they could use. For 10,000 years Plains Indians maintained the same roving lifestyle; a rhythm of season, rich with tradition, love and respect for the land and all of its creatures. They left behind teepee and fire rings, tools, petroglyphs and pictographs—a living history lying on the prairie topsoil. The Comanche, Kiowa, Cheyenne, Arapaho and Apache tribes of the Colorado plains understood drought, severe winters and the importance of fire—harmony in a land where there is no balance.

A school lesson is etched in my memory, about bison and the Indians, and pictures from a textbook showing people leaning out of a train, shooting bison. I never understood how that could happen.

Many things led to the extirpation of the

FACING PAGE: Bison bull silhouette, Buffalo Groves Ranch.
INSET: 1,000-year-old bison bone and carving tools,
discovered along First Creek in Rocky Mountain Arsenal NWR.

American prairie bison from the Great Plains: buffalo hide and tongue hunters; an unwritten U.S. policy to exterminate bison to starve the Indians; cattle herds being driven through grazing lands to market; and use of bison meat to feed railroad workers. The railroad became the transport for green "buffalo" hides to drive machinery in eastern factories, the last straw for American prairie bison. For decades their bleached bones covered the plains. Most of the bison were slaughtered in just two decades. By 1884, the American prairie bison was nearly extinct.

The effort to save the remaining bison was nothing short of heroic, a defining time for North American conservation. From 1873 to 1889, six men captured 88 bison that remained on the North American plains. Charles "Buffalo" Jones, Frederic Dupree, Walking Coyote, Charles Goodnight, Charles Alloway and James McKay each had their own reasons for saving the disappearing species; some had a pure vision of saving bison from extinction and others saw possible business opportunities. The last recorded sighting of bison near Denver was in 1883, six animals near land later occupied by Rocky Mountain Arsenal. With the exception of the Yellowstone herd, all Plains bison are descendants of the original 88 animals.

In 1905, Bronx Zoo biologist William Hornaday convinced Teddy Roosevelt and others to found the American Bison Society for "the permanent preservation and increase of the American bison." As honorary society president, Roosevelt gained approval from Congress to establish wildlife preserves and teamed up with private bison owners to stock the preserves and parks. By 1929, the American prairie bison numbered 3,385 animals.

There are more than 400,000 bison spread out over private and public lands today. Of those, about 10,000 have no genetic cattle markers—they are nearly genetically pure. These "pure" bison are spread out over numerous sites managed by the U.S. Fish and Wildlife Service in order to achieve genetic diversity. The return of bison from the brink of extinction is, without question, one of our greatest conservation achievements.

I offer this brief historical perspective for several reasons. It is nearly impossible to discuss the Great Plains without talking about bison, magnificent creatures ingrained in our Western heritage, and a Plains keystone species that plays a major role in the health of the grasslands. Native Americans place a high spiritual value on bison, considering them a link to the past and vital to native cultures. We will never see millions of bison roaming the Great Plains again, but I believe we are obligated to ask, "What is the future of bison on the Great Plains?"

Springtime on the Pawnee.
INSET: Bison cow and calf.

40

41

Bison cow and calf at rest.

FACING PAGE: A massive bull bison.

A dust bowl relic near Hereford in Weld County.

# Homesteading and the Dust Bowl

*Black Sunday - On April 14, 1935,the biggest dust storm ever to rage across southeastern Colorado billowed several miles high. The sun was completely blotted out and skies were dark for 24 hours. Because of the Great Depression and the Dust Bowl, many families had no choice but to abandon their homesteads.*
—from a sign on the Comanche National Grasslands

Human history and natural history are permanently intertwined on the grasslands. Ghost houses from the *Dirty Thirties* still dot the landscape, their wood shingle roofs and plaster walls rattling in the wind. They are mostly stick houses—one-room shacks and dilapidated two-story homes that can be seen for miles. Whenever I see one of these dust bowl icons, I can't resist stepping inside. I stand still and listen, trying to get a feel for the isolation, the long winters and unrelenting wind, the blazing summer heat, the joy of a wet spring, and the desperation of the dust bowl years that the original tenants experienced. Homesteading the western plains started in the 1880s with sod-busters claiming land and building sod huts. The bigger homesteading push came at the start of the 20th Century, with a Jeffersonian

Egli Family portrait.

vision to bring agriculture to a land that should arguably never have been turned over. Any 21-year-old willing to "prove up" could claim a piece of the American west. Yeomen tilled under the remaining bleached bones of bison as the deep roots of native grasses cracked and popped beneath the plow.

Dick and Sandra Tanner are fifth-generation ranchers on the Bohart Ranch, near Yoder in El Paso County. The ranch was managed by the Tanners when it was purchased by The Nature Conservancy, who in turn sold the land to the Colorado State Land Board. TNC holds the grazing lease.

The Bohart is a sprawling landscape of rolling prairie with a commanding view of Pikes Peak, and home to more than 100 bird species and a thriving pronghorn herd. Grass is the Tanner's inventory, and on the subject of conservation, Dick and Sandra like to say, "We were conservationists before there was a name for it." It was here that Sandra's great-grandparents, Charles and Minnie Gieck homesteaded on a half-section in 1914. With no water on the land, Charles would hitch up a wagon at 3:00a.m. every day to gather water for the ranch. The nearest supplies were in Calhan, a three day round trip. (Underground streams provide water today.)

Homesteaders were also claiming land near Denver on what is now Rocky Mountain Arsenal National Wildlife Refuge. I met with Lucille Egli-McIntyre and Ernie Mauer, who grew up in homestead families on arsenal land. Gottleib Egli emigrated from Switzerland in 1912 and homesteaded on arsenal land, not far from Denver, which is where he met Lucille's mother, Rose. Ernie Mauer's parents came to Colorado in 1903 after Ernie's great-uncle, Gottleib Miller, wrote the family and said the Colorado prairie was "the land of milk and honey". After the family sold all of their possessions, sailed on the U.S.S. Philadelphia to Ellis Island, and transferred to Denver, the great-uncle took them to his sod hut near Sable and Smith Road. There he had one cow—his land of milk and honey.

The arsenal land was settled by immigrant farmers, many of them Swiss. Swiss dances were big occasions, with men and boys in suits and women and girls donning dresses. Kids attended Rose School, a four-room schoolhouse with two grades in each room. The only business on arsenal land was Big Ed's Bar, a shot-and-a-beer basement establishment.

The Eglis grew corn and alfalfa, and were mostly self-sufficient, with a garden, cows and chickens. Over time, Gottleib amassed 1,000 acres by buying land from farmer's who couldn't pay their taxes. In addition to eight kids, the Eglis had hired hands to work the farm and Lucille's mom served three home-cooked meals a day for 12 or more people on the back porch.

I wanted to know firsthand about the dust bowl of the Dirty Thirties. Lucille was too young to remember, but Ernie recalled the thick dust clouds and his mother using a scoop shovel to remove dirt that had seeped through windows into the kitchen. There were no crops for two years, and in 1932 a good bean crop was ruined before the Mauers could stack and transport the crop to market. The Eglis and Mauers managed to get through the dust bowl with their gardens, chickens and cows. They were fortunate to have irrigation water from the Farmer's Highline Canal, the difference in a battle to survive.

The environmental and social catastrophe of the dust bowl was a result of decades of over-grazing and the plowing up of lands bound by native grasses. Drought is part of the normal cycle here and did not cause the blinding dust clouds rising to 12,000 feet. The dust bowl was purely a human-caused disaster. Sandra Tanner, with her five-generations-on-the-land perspective, told me that the drought from 2002 to 2004 was worse than the dust bowl years. In *Grassland*, Richard Manning wrote, "Indeed it was an enormous upheaval, but to blame it, as many do, on drought is to blame the spark and not the fuel. Drought is as normal to the plains as floods are to the Mississippi and fire is to California's chaparral. Periodic drought is not an aberration but the norm on arid land."

In 1933, with desperate ranchers feeding prickly pear cactus to cattle, their children freezing in unheated shacks, the federal government began purchasing failed crop lands under the National Industrial Act and Emergency Relief Appropriations Act. Called Land Utilization Projects, these efforts enabled families to start a new life somewhere else, while retiring thousands of farms from cultivation. Initially managed by the U.S. Department of Agriculture, the lands were turned over to the U.S. Forest Service in 1954 and were established as National Grasslands in 1960. Today, the maps of the Pawnee and Comanche National Grasslands look like a mosaic of private and public lands because of the way the tracts were purchased.

Distant Pikes Peak caps this expansive view of the Front Range from the Bohart Ranch in El Paso County. INSET: A weathered window reflects prairie light.

Harvest time in the land of milk and honey.

Harvester gears.

Broken dreams.

FOLLOWING PAGES: Yuma County homestead.

# Prairie Summer

One blazing summer afternoon, with temperatures in the mid-90's, I drove north up Interstate-25 on my way to the Pawnee National Grassland. Traveling with no particular agenda, as I often do, I headed towards the Wyoming border and took a right at Rockport, just shy of the Chalk Bluffs.

With towering cumulus clouds building in my rear view mirror, the world changed as soon as I left the interstate. Lark buntings and vesper sparrows burst from grass to fence post, then back again, mocking my attempts to make a photograph. Small bands of male pronghorn tolerated my presence in the vehicle, while females with fawns fled immediately. I spotted a nighthawk on a fencepost, investigated badger burrows and marveled at Swainson's hawk fledglings circling overhead, nearly ready for their return trip to Argentina.

Clouds twisted in artistic shapes over the Chalk Bluffs, better than any Impressionist painting, while more serious storm clouds drifted across the Wyoming border.

That evening, the Pawnee Buttes lit up like coals as the sun dropped behind the Rockies, eventually disappearing into a prairie night. I lingered for awhile, soaking up the warmth on an evening that I'll never forget.

Rocky Mountain bee plant flourishes on the Pawnee in summer.

American white pelicans reflected in Lake Derby,
Rocky Mountain Arsenal NWR.

TOP: A two- or three-day-old pronghorn fawn is tucked in tall grass
as the mother grazes—and watches—nearby. Like deer, pronghorn fawns
are born nearly scentless until they can outrun a coyote within a week.

BOTTOM: A pronghorn buck and doe, Pawnee National Grassland.

An aerial view of the South Platte River, east of Greeley. From its headwaters in the Rocky Mountains to its confluence with the North Platte River in Nebraska, it provides vital riparian habitat for a wide range of species, including sandhill and whooping cranes. From the air, one can see the many channels of the river and surrounding cottonwood forest.

A raptor's-eye view of the Pawnee Buttes, an important nesting site
for a variety of birds of prey. With good spring rains, the land will stay green into mid-June.

Cowpen daisies bloom below a massive cottonwood tree in fog,
Rocky Mountain Arsenal NWR.

TOP: Blazing stars are brilliant late-bloomers,
flowering at the end of August, after the summer monsoon.

BOTTOM: Commercial sunflower farm at sunrise, near Erie.

Cormorants and sunrise fog at Rocky Mountain Arsenal NWR.

TOP: A photographer's cover is blown.

BOTTOM: A large brood of nine burrowing owl chicks on alert for predators.
The species is state-threatened.

Cherry Creek spills over ledges in Castlewood Canyon.

LEFT: Expansive skies over Lake Gulch,
Castlewood Canyon State Park, Douglas County.

Rocky Mountain Arsenal south entrance, circa 1960.

# WAR

On a typical early-summer day in June of 1942, the immigrant pioneers of pre-Rocky Mountain Arsenal land were told that the government needed their land for the war and they would be evicted. A May *Rocky Mountain News* headline had announced that a chemical weapons plant was coming to Denver. The escalation of World War II and a growing chemical weapons threat led to the creation of Rocky Mountain Arsenal on the outskirts of Denver. The location was close to a major metropolitan area, with a pool of skilled labor, near railroad lines, and perhaps most important, had a reliable water source in Lake Ladora, a lake built by the settlers for irrigation. The Army moved quickly and seized the land within a few weeks.

In *Twenty-Seven Square Miles*, author John F. Hoffecker wrote of the time, "First the site would have to be cleared. Everyone living on the land within the boundaries of the new Arsenal would have to leave almost immediately. Within weeks, the federal government seized the land under condemnation proceedings (filed in the U.S. District Court on June 15), and the hundreds of families on the site were forced to abandon their homes. By all accounts, most did so without protest, but the pain of the experience was never forgotten. Robert Moffitt recalls that he was notified by mail, and learned that he had thirteen days to move out (although he later obtained several extensions and was actually one of the last to leave). On the day of their departure in July, the Egli children recalled that their father—a strong and taciturn Swiss—sat down and wept."

Lucille Egli-McIntyre confirmed the story and told me that her family left when the corn was six feet high; one of the best summers ever. Rather than allowing the farmers to harvest the crops, they were left in the fields to rot. The arsenal farmers waited up to nine months to be paid by the Army for their land. The Eglis lived with Lucille's sister Gladys for a time while they waited for payment. The Mauers bought five acres near 62nd and Monaco. Payments varied by the amount of land, and those with smaller plots were paid just one dollar.

The Army quickly constructed a 260-acre core industrial complex, and civilian workers produced the first batch of mustard gas on New Year's Day, 1943. While producing tons of poisonous gas, the Army was changing strategy and a petroleum bomb plant was added to the burgeoning weapons facility. The arsenal was running around the clock to meet the demand for millions of bombs. The German city of Hamburg and the ball-bearing plants of Schweinfurt would be wiped out by tons of petroleum fire bombs built at Rocky Mountain Arsenal. The arsenal also served a dual role as a prisoner-of-war camp, while incendiaries were dropped in Europe and Japan, playing a major role in deciding the war. Sixteen square miles of Tokyo were burned in one night, as 80,000 people were killed by arsenal bombs.

In June of 1944, General William N. Porter, commander of the Chemical Warfare Service, visited Rocky Mountain Arsenal to recognize employees for their contribution to the war effort. Weapons construction was winding down.

In addition to mustard gas, napalm and petroleum incendiaries, Rocky Mountain Arsenal employees went on to produce deadly sarin gas in a secret facility (building 1501) during the Cold War. Next to Henderson Hill, a former Indian lookout, was the north plant; a 25-million-dollar sarin gas facility manned by workers in rubber suits—one of which appeared on the front page of the *Rocky Mountain News* on March 20, 1954. In the '60s, rice blast spores (a type of germ weapon) were stored and cultivated at the arsenal, and "button bombs" were being shipped to southeast Asia during the Vietnam War. Because of its close chemical composition to mustard gas, Shell Corporation also manufactured pesticide on the site.

Under President Richard Nixon, who condemned the use of chemical weapons, Rocky Mountain Arsenal changed direction and began destroying its stockpile of weaponry in 1969, although production would not completely cease until 1982. After four decades of producing some of the most toxic substances known to Man, the once-native prairie was a very polluted place. In 1984, the commander of Rocky Mountain Arsenal, Lieutenant Colonel Richard W. Smith, called the industrial core "the most contaminated square mile in the nation." Some called it "the most contaminated tract of real estate on planet Earth."

In *Silent Spring*, Rachel Carson wrote, "In 1943, the Rocky Mountain Arsenal of the Army Chemical Corps, located near Denver, began to manufacture war materials. Eight years later the facilities of the Arsenal were leased to a private oil company for the production of insecticides. Even before the change of operations, however, mysterious reports had begun to come in. Farmers several miles from the plant began to report unexplained sickness among livestock, they complained of extensive crop damage. Foliage turned yellow, plants failed to mature, and many crops were killed outright. There were reports of human illness, thought by some to be related."

# Rocky Mountain Arsenal National Wildlife Refuge

Bordered on three sides by residential areas, Rocky Mountain Arsenal was viewed as a toxic wasteland by an increasingly dubious public. Colorado Congresswoman Pat Schroeder was a very vocal critic at the time, and the U.S. Army was facing the monumental task of cleaning up 40 years of toxins.

In the early stages of cleanup, 20 endangered bald eagles were discovered roosting on arsenal land. (Legend has it that biologist Mike Lockhart made the discovery.) On the heels of this remarkable find, photographers Wendy Shattil and Bob Rozinsky visited the arsenal in 1988 and reported "staggering numbers of birds and mammals, including eagles, hawks, owls, deer, coyotes, prairie dogs, and others," The undeveloped land surrounding the arsenal facilities had served as an urban refuge throughout the 40 years of industrialization.

With Congresswoman Schroeder pushing for an accelerated cleanup, the wild discoveries led to a plan to set aside Rocky Mountain Arsenal as a National Wildlife Refuge. The first President Bush signed *The Rocky Mountain Arsenal National Wildlife Refuge Act* into law in 1992. The U.S. Army and Shell Corporation have partnered and honored their commitment to the American people by continuing to clean up "the most contaminated square mile in the nation" for nearly a quarter century. As I write this, the cleanup is nearly complete—visitors fish in Lakes Ladora and Mary, and bison have dropped three calves this spring. A dedicated U.S. Fish and Wildlife Service staff has managed the recovery of wildlife and grassland while striving for an exceptional visitor experience. The refuge has traveled full circle from native prairie and Indian hunting camp to homestead farmland, chemical weapons facility, toxic wasteland, and back to native prairie.

FACING PAGE: Bald eagle in flight.
INSET: Male western meadowlark in song.

Prairie grass and fog at sunrise.
INSET: White-tail fawn hidden in grass.

Swainson's hawk adult perched in spring catkins.

April marks the arrival of the Swainson's hawk to nesting sites in central and western North America. This signature raptor of the shortgrass prairie travels a remarkable 14,000 miles from wintering grounds on the pampas of Brazil and Argentina. The annual migration takes up to two months! Easily identified by their reddish chest "bib," this large buteo feeds on a wide variety of prey, from insects to small mammals. Population declines have been tied to pesticides used in South America. In spring and early summer, Swainson's build or add to existing nests, mate, and raise their young (males help with incubation), in preparation for their return to South America in September. Swainson's remind us that we are a world prairie!

Black-tailed prairie dogs.

Considered a prairie keystone species, the black-tailed prairie dog is one of five species of prairie dog found in North America. Viewed as pests since the plains were settled, black-tailed prairie dog habitat and populations have been reduced to two percent of their historic range. Called dogs by French explorers for their barking behavior, these burrowing rodents provide food and shelter for a wide variety of indigenous creatures, including eagles, hawks, burrowing owls, black-footed ferrets, swift foxes, insects, snakes, salamanders, toads and small rodents. Through their excavation activity, they raise nutrients to the top soil level, benefitting bison and livestock. Prairie dog towns are actually complex ecosystems at the heart of a healthy shortgrass prairie. Black-tailed prairie dogs are also considered a species of concern by the Colorado Division of Wildlife.

Canada geese in flight.

Male redhead duck in
a prairie wetland.

# Extinct!

Grassland conservation reached a critical crossroads in 1979. As production was winding down at Rocky Mountain Arsenal, greater prairie chickens were threatened, the bald eagle was listed as endangered because of widespread DDT use, and after 15 years on the endangered species list, the black-footed ferret was declared extinct. North America's only native ferret had fallen victim to habitat loss and disease.

Two years later, in tiny Meeteetse, Wyoming, a pair of ranch dogs named Shep and Scarface made an unlikely discovery. Shep caught a black-footed ferret and brought home evidence that the animals still existed in the wild. That set off a remarkable chain of events as biologists descended on Meeteetse and discovered more than 120 wild ferrets. Eighteen individuals were captured, and a historic recovery program ensued.

My experience photographing ferrets was at the first-class National Black-Footed Ferret Conservation Center on the plains north of Wellington, Colorado. The facility is managed by the same Mike Lockhart who, legend has it, discovered the arsenal eagles. Biologists in clean room suits raise ferrets in four large breeding rooms, and new arrivals are checked for disease in the quarantine room. Outside, 48 pens house up to ten ferrets each as they learn the necessary skills for survival in the wild. The ferrets live in burrows and learn to prey on prairie dogs, starting out with *pieces* of prairie dogs.

I observed and laughed out loud as one particularly gregarious ferret leaped, spun in the air, and raced from burrow to burrow, daring me to capture his antics with camera and lens. Fortunately, he stopped and observed me occasionally, and I had the thrill of photographing our most endangered mammal.

Black-footed ferrets are almost completely dependant on prairie dogs for survival. Nocturnal by nature, their camouflage enables them to blend into the prairie landscape while they live and raise their young in burrows and feed on prairie dogs. Black-footed ferrets are mustelids, or musk-producing mammals, a family that includes badgers, mink, skunks, martens, fishers, weasels, wolverines, polecats and domestic ferrets. Their elongated bodies and pronounced claws make them perfectly suited for travel through underground burrows, while their large heads, powerful jaws and sharp teeth allow them to crush bone. Including tail, a black-footed ferret is 18-24 inches long.

More than 2,200 ferrets have been released into the wild since 1991, with roughly 1,000 living on wild grasslands today. Although the numbers are impressive from the brink of extinction, quality re-introduction sites are the key for stabilizing, and fully recovering the species. Black-footed ferrets are highly susceptible to plague and canine distemper. As Mike Lockhart explained, at a minimum, ten quality sites and 1,500 pre-breeding adults are required to down-list black-footed ferrets from *federally endangered* to *threatened*, and to ensure a healthy wild population. Ferrets need large prairie dog complexes, or "towns," to thrive, which is what landed them on the endangered species list in 1964. Prairie dogs have been reduced to one percent of their range and remain hated and misunderstood by many. In the Conata Basin of South Dakota, the prairie dogs that support the largest wild population of black-footed ferrets are slated to be poisoned by our government in October, 2007. It's a strange feeling writing this piece, not knowing if conservationists will be able to save our best black-footed ferret release site. It is disconcerting, to say the least, knowing that the future of this magnificent creature can be determined by a politician's pen.

Of the ten sites in the world currently suitable for black-footed ferrets, none exist on Colorado's shortgrass prairie, but potential "nursery" sites are being considered. The species is doing well at Dinosaur National Monument in the northwest part of the state.

As I was leaving the Conservation Center with an autumn storm blowing in and temperatures plummeting, the ferrets that I had just photographed were being trapped for release into the wild.

## LISTEN TO THE BIRDS

If we care to listen, birds will tell us about the health of grasslands. Recent news from the Colorado Audubon Society isn't good. The summer, 2007, press release, *Common Birds In Decline*, was splashed across local and national papers, including the *Denver Post* and *New York Times*. The report lists four of the five common birds in decline: Lark bunting, Colorado's State Bird, down 64% in 40 years; western meadowlark, down 71%; northern harrier, down 77%; and horned lark, historically our most abundant bird, down 72%. The data was compiled using the Christmas Bird Count and the U.S. Geological Survey's breeding bird survey. Front Range sprawl, road fragmentation and agricultural pressure have reduced quality habitat in direct proportion to the avian decline.

These common birds aren't currently at risk of landing on the Endangered Species List, but their losses are alarming. Carol Browner, Audubon Chairperson and former EPA Administrator, explained, "Their decline tells us we have serious work to do, from protecting local habitats to addressing the huge threats from global warming."

The good news is that Audubon has created the Important Bird Area (IBA) program and identified 55 IBAs across the state. Audubon casts a wide net across Colorado as member volunteers participate in bird monitoring projects, determining population trends. The "Adopt an IBA" program promotes local conservation and IBA information influences future land management and development decisions.

The sobering reality of declining bird populations is tempered by their relatively large numbers where quality habitat exists. Through education and involvement at many levels, we can improve habitat and help birds to rebound.

Birds of the prairie ~
TOP ROW: House finch; yellow-headed blackbird; lark bunting.
MIDDLE ROW: mountain bluebird; red-winged blackbird; vesper sparrow.
BOTTOM ROW: Western meadowlark; mountain plover; American tree sparrow.

FACING PAGE: Roosting bald eagles silhouetted at sunrise.

# Prairie Autumn

*No spring nor summer beauty hath such grace
as I have seen in one autumnal face.*
— John Donne

A shortgrass prairie anomaly lies in the shadow of the Flatirons, near Boulder. A strip of xeric (dry) tallgrass prairie, four miles wide at most, is sandwiched between foothills to the west and shortgrass to the east. The land leading up to the pediment-top mesas of Rocky Flats *designated* National Wildlife Refuge (former manufacturing site for plutonium triggers for nuclear weaponry) receives slightly more rain than the eastern plains. Glacial cobble near the surface traps moisture in the soil, allowing for big bluestem and Indian grass to thrive here. The autumn grasses turn a brilliant red, contrasted with golden cottonwoods along the stream banks and drainages. Ironically, the glacial cobble that created the tallgrass habitat saved the land from the plow.

Autumn grasses, heavy with seed, begin their change to a tapestry of color before we notice the passing of summer. Late-blooming blazing star wildflowers carpet the grassland in white as mulies and whitetail deer shed their velvet. Burrowing owls and Swainson's hawks depart on their long journeys south, as another remarkable cycle of migration takes flight.

The crack of antlers crashing together is serious business, pronghorn and deer settling the age-old question of superiority. Throughout the November rut, bucks fight for the right to mate in a brutal ritual that has gone on since the birth of the species. Rocky Mountain Arsenal bison will rut for the first time in 125 years this year. That will be something to see!

As days shorten, nights cool and cottonwoods drop their leaves, the first bald eagles arrive from Yukon Territory and Alaska. They will stay until February or March, feeding on black-tailed prairie dogs and fish, if there is open water.

Flicker feather and fallen leaves.

FACING PAGE: Autumn poplars at Eldorado Canyon State Park.

Cottonwood in snow on Marshall Mesa, Boulder Open Space.

Cottonwood trees and meadow at Garden of the Gods, Colorado Springs.

Sumac turns brilliant red below the Flatirons near Boulder.

The last rays of sun graze Ogalalla capstone on
an October evening at The Nature Conservancy's
Fox Ranch in Yuma County.

A northern harrier in flight.

A massive mule deer buck tastes the air to determine if
the female he is pursuing is ready to mate during the fall rut,
Rocky Mountain Arsenal NWR.

FOLLOWING PAGES: The Indian Peaks provide backdrop for
a sky full of Canada geese, Rocky Mountain Arsenal NWR.

A strong autumn storm signals a change of seasons in Boulder Open Space.

FACING PAGE: Juniper snags catch the last rays of sun at Apishapa Canyon State Wildlife Area. The canyon is home to many native species, including bighorn sheep.

# Buffalo Commons

The Great Plains agricultural community was turned on its ear in 1987, when Rutgers University professors Frank and Debra Popper published *Buffalo Commons*, a proposal that many viewed as a threat to the very underpinnings of the prairie way of life. Others simply thought it was crazy.

Buffalo Commons, as the name implies, suggests that reintroduction of free-roaming bison herds will aid in restoring the ecological and social health of the plains. With native bird populations in decline, aquifers, rivers and streams being drained beyond sustainable levels, and rural towns drying up because of "out-migration," the Poppers proposed a "large-scale land restoration project."

Grasslands are healthiest when grazed and trampled by large, nomadic creatures, stirring up the land and bringing other animals with them. Grazed land encourages growth and diversity of native grasses at the expense of invasive species. American prairie bison, in constant motion, finding water where there is none, grazing, rolling and flowing across the prairie, evolved with native grasses from the gargantuan Pleistocene *Bison antiquus* to become the quintessential prairie beast. They are almost a talisman of the plains.

It is not surprising that ranchers and environmentalists were polarized on both sides of the discussion, and ranchers weren't volunteering to tear down fences and raise bison in common areas. Regardless of which side you choose, there is no denying that native creatures, particularly birds, are in sharp decline, and rural communities are dying as young people leave and those who stay are aging. Present tense is appropriate here, because that is still the case today.

Dave and Marlene Groves run the Buffalo Groves Ranch near Kiowa, their own smaller version of a Buffalo Commons. Give or take, 100 head of bison roam their high ponderosa savannah overlooking the entire Front Range. From their humble beginnings with four head in their Elizabeth backyard, the Groves have grown into a premier bison ranch. The animals eat only grass—native buffalo and blue grama grass with no invasive cheat and crested wheat grasses. The landscape, with bison silhouetted against the sky, is stunning. In the winter of 2006-2007, the hardest winter anyone can recall, the Groves did not lose a single animal—bison are that resilient. Marlene even saw two of these athletic beasts leap over the side of a stock tank to break ice!

A vast expanse of Fremont playa in Lincoln County.
INSET: Long-billed curlew
FACING PAGE: Wind turbine farm and waves of wheat, Pawnee National Grassland

# A New Conservation Model

**W**inds of change are blowing across the central grasslands today and Colorado is in the center of the shifting landscape. In October of 2006, a diverse group of conservationists, private land owners and representatives of various government agencies met at The Nature Conservancy's Fox Ranch in Yuma County. They were there to discuss the Central Shortgrass Prairie Ecoregional Assessment and Partnership Initiative (CSP), a plan to build alliances for a sustainable prairie and a conservation implementation strategy. I met many of the folks at the meeting and was thunderstruck by the civility and positive atmosphere. I went along on a tour of the ranch and learned about the fragility of the Arickaree River and its importance as a ribbon of tallgrass prairie and cottonwood gallery forest. Water flows on the Arickaree fluctuate with the drawdown of the Ogallala aquifer, our threatened (and shrinking) underground lake.

The CSP Assessment Report and Executive Summary have since been released. The report is a tome that openly acknowledges that grasslands are one of North America's most imperiled ecosystems, that "grassland birds have exhibited the most severe and extensive declines of any other class of North American species," and that "key prairie species, such as the mountain plover and black-tailed prairie dog, have declined." At the same time, the report paints an optimistic picture for the future, stating that "due in large part to land-use patterns and past stewardship practices on private and public lands, approximately 50% of the ecoregion remains in a predominantly natural condition."

The ecoregion covers approximately 56 million acres of the western Great Plains, including parts of Colorado, Kansas, Nebraska, New Mexico, Oklahoma, Texas and Wyoming. We are indeed part of a much larger grassland community. The detail of the report is astonishing, with identification and mapping of "146 animal and plant species that are state and/or federally listed, or are considered imperiled, endemic, or declining." Black-tailed

prairie dog communities, natural plant and riparian areas and shorebird aggregation areas are all identified in the CSP. Climate and socioeconomic trends are also discussed in great detail.

Threats to biodiversity include housing and urban development, increased road density, energy development, altered hydrology (wells, dams and diversions), invasive species (considered by many to pose the biggest threat), and climate change (global warming).

Global warming threatens to permanently alter life on the shortgrass prairie in ways that we are only beginning to comprehend. Writing for *Audubon Magazine*, author Robert H. Boyle says the earth could be three degrees Fahrenheit warmer by the year 2050. "It has not been that hot for 200,000 years, a time well before humans evolved." He goes on to say that "climate zones could shift 400 miles north by the end of the next century."

Wind energy is exploding across the plains—development on a massive scale. Surprisingly, wind energy—good for everyone, a win-win, right?—threatens to fragment fragile habitats and alter migration routes if not managed properly. Although wind turbines have been improved to make sure their massive blades are less likely to kill raptors and bats, their physical presence can cause nesting and mating problems for sensitive grassland birds. Accordingly, conservation groups and agencies, led by Audubon Colorado, encourage developers to conduct pre-development assessments at turbine and distribution sites, use that information to limit the impact of these developments on sensitive species, and monitor the potential impact following wind facility development.

What is important for most of us to know is that The Nature Conservancy (TNC) has assumed a leadership role in bringing people together to create a sustainable grassland, a place where our generation *and* future generations can experience the wonders of the western Great Plains. The Nature Conservancy is one of many organizations participating in the Shortgrass Prairie Partnership that works toward this common goal. The rate of conservation via conservation easements, promotion of land management practices, creative thinking and spirit of partnership is unprecedented. The top conservation strategy is working in partnership with private landowners, who own 90% of the Central Shortgrass Prairie.

Through TNC and the Rocky Mountain Bird Observatory, I recently visited the Stogsdill Ranch near Karval, in Lincoln County. Carl and Cherry Stogsdill have been recognized by the Colorado Division of Wildlife (CDOW) as Colorado Wildlife Landowners of the Year for their exemplary stewardship of the land. Sitting at their kitchen table, I learned that swift fox density is so high on their land that the CDOW traps the foxes for reintroduction to South Dakota. Thirty-five of the cat-sized foxes were trapped in a single night! The Stogsdills are part of the Colorado Birding Trail, volunteer landowners who allow private citizens on their land to view wildlife. Visitors pay a nominal fee to see mountain plovers, burrowing owls, swift foxes, pronghorn and other native species. The Stogsdills are founders of the new Karval Mountain Plover Festival, held in May, a chance for folks to view and learn about this imperiled creature. It is also a vehicle to restore pride and bring tourism to a small town in decline. The Karval festival follows the examples of the Wray greater prairie chicken tours and the Lamar snow goose festival in seeking eco-tourists.

I was there mostly to photograph a playa, a prairie wetland lake that holds water for brief periods and provides vital shorebird and migratory bird habitat. We toured the rolling terrain in my small pickup, traveling through expansive prairie dog towns populated with horned larks, meadowlarks and burrowing owls. We ran into some CDOW biologists who were counting burrowing owls that day. Rounding a turn and looking at a barren area which Carl said is good for plovers, we saw a pair mating. Carl jumped up, his cowboy hat hitting the ceiling of my little truck, and exclaimed "plovers mating!" I still chuckle to think that this man, who has lived here his entire life, was probably more excited than I was. Carl was generous with his time, showing me wet and dry playas. In the late afternoon, passing a derelict dust bowl two-story, I went down to the Fremont playa, a 47-acre "super-playa" nestled in rolling hills. Walking the shoreline, grousing about the mud threatening my shoe-tops, I looked up to see a long-billed curlew had landed on the playa. He was using his elongated, curved beak to stir up food, while strutting in shallow water, clay mud dripping each time he raised a foot. Playas are called "jewels of the plains," small depressions lined with clay that attract wildlife and are the primary recharge source for the Ogallala aquifer. There are 60,000 known playas on the central plains, the most important and critically threatened wetlands in the eco-region.

A two-and-a-half-hour drive home gave me time to think about eco-tourism, the Colorado Birding Trail, landowner partnerships—the whole business. Carl and Cherry had said things started to change about five years ago when Ken Morgan became the CDOW liaison and landowners began to trust the Division of Wildlife. In a Patagonia catalog environmental essay, Theodore Roosevelt IV wrote, "Environmentalists are looking at a hard-pressed rural America and asking, 'What can you give us?,' instead of standing with rural people in their view shed to understand their problems and build strong, durable alliances that are partisanship-proof." That is the heart and soul of what is changing in Colorado.

A swift fox patrols the Pawnee night.
Called "ghosts of the plains," swift foxes are mostly nocturnal,
and considered a species of concern by the Colorado Division of Wildlife.

Arickaree River tallgrass and beaver-chewed cottonwood tree
on The Nature Conservancy's Fox Ranch, Yuma County.

# Prairie Winter

Beautifully monochromatic, a hush falls over the plains under the first snows. The sound of snow falling on grass is perfectly out of place in today's bustle. While the snow is falling, one may see a grazing deer or pronghorn, and bison simply go about their business. Canada geese and howling coyote packs seem to be the only creatures bold enough to crack the silence.

Winter storms can be fierce, and the plains don't suffer fools. I learned this firsthand when I drove out to the Pawnee in hopes of capturing a winter sunrise. I augured into a wind-crusted drift and wound up digging myself out with a snowshoe that happened to be in the back of my truck. One year prior, I was in shirt sleeves making pictures around the buttes and lamenting the lack of snow.

It is a season of grass coated in hoarfrost and dendritic shapes of cottonwoods, ferruginous hawks roosting in prairie dog towns and northern harriers coasting just a few feet above the grassland.

Winter is the miracle of wildlife adapting to the most severe conditions on the plains—a race against the clock, waiting for a dormant land to spring to life.

Big bluestem grasses in snow.

FACING PAGE: A lone tree braves life on windswept hillsides in Jefferson County.

A spectacular winter sunrise over Lake Ladora,
Rocky Mountain Arsenal NWR.

LEFT: Wave clouds crest over peaks of the
northern Front Range. Clearly visible are
the Flatirons in Boulder and Longs Peak,
the high point of Rocky Mountain National Park.

95

TOP: Bison running in snow, Denver herd.

BOTTOM: Snow and saltbrush, Pawnee National Grassland.

FACING PAGE: Clearing storm over the Flatirons, Boulder Open Space.

TOP: Ferruginous hawk with rabbit kill.

BOTTOM: Early winter snow blankets the grassland near Vogel Canyon,
Comanche National Grassland.

LEFT: A red fox in late winter coat pauses in golden grasses
along the Wheat Ridge Greenbelt, Jefferson County.

RIGHT: An impressive mule deer buck at Rocky Mountain Arsenal NWR.

# Piñon Canyon Controversy

The U.S. Army currently occupies a 238,000-acre area south of La Junta, called the Piñon Canyon Military Maneuver Site. Although the Army uses live ammunition on the site, they have made an effort to be a good conservation partner by purchasing conservation easements from willing sellers to protect native grasslands and rare native plants, and to buffer the site from the encroachment of development. Most of the conservation easements have been with local ranchers who continue to own and graze their land. To date, the Army has conserved nearly 10,000 acres, with another 8,000 on the way. A long section of the Purgatoire River flows through the site—juniper-studded bluffs rising above the plains. It is bordered by centennial cattle ranches and the Timpas (northern) unit of Comanche National Grassland.

Between La Junta and Kim, Highway-109 skirts around the Timpas unit of the Comanche and the Army's land. Signs stating "THIS LAND NOT FOR SALE TO THE ARMY" stand in front of every ranch on the rolling route, passing the turnoff for Vogel and Picketwire Canyons, and across the chocolate Purgatoire River, while gaining elevation to juniper savannah.

The signs protest the Army's plan to "acquire" an additional 418,000 acres adjacent to the existing land. They claim the acreage is needed to fire long-range weapons and train new troops. When the Army "acquired" land in 1983, they used eminent domain and promised to never shoot live ammo and never increase the size of the maneuver site. Live ammunition is currently used on the site, and now the Army wants more land—promises broken. Rumors abound that the Army really wants 2.5 *million* acres, essentially all of southeast Colorado, including the Comanche National Grassland.

This is canyon and cattle country, a land so sparsely populated that parts could qualify as wilderness. Southeast Colorado is defined by extremes—the snowstorms in the winter of 2006-2007 were some of the worst in recorded history, when back-to-back blizzards covered the plains under four feet of snow. Thousands of cattle died. The drought years of 2002 and 2003 brought 3.5 inches of rain *total* to the area. It is also a fragile landscape at the heart of the '30s dust bowl. Sound grazing practices and good land management prevented the topsoil from blowing away during the recent drought.

The Comanche is separated into two units, north and south, the Timpas and Corrizo, respectively. Managed by the U.S. Forest Service, the canyons house important archeological sites, pictographs and petroglyphs, and in Picketwire Canyon, the

FACING PAGE: Frontier cemetary in Picketwire Canyon, Comanche National Grassland.
INSET: Allosaurus track preserved in an ancient seabed.

most important dinosaur track site in North America. Native wildlife includes the threatened lesser prairie chicken, large prairie dog ecosystems and associated species, nesting shortgrass prairie songbirds, pronghorn, even roadrunners. Relatively speaking, the area is as important to the shortgrass prairie as Rocky Mountain National Park is to the mountains.

In a *Rocky Mountain News* article, local rancher Kevin Karney said, "There's ranchers out there who you could offer any amount of money, and they'll say no." The unified ranching community has led the way for a complete rejection of the expansion. With no support for the expansion from Colorado legislators, an amendment to a defense appropriations bill denying the Army of money needed to acquire additional Piñon Canyon land was overwhelmingly adopted in Congress. It appears that the Comanche and surrounding private lands have been saved from the indignation of land seizure for now.

The southeast ranchers will certainly keep a watchful eye on the Army's political maneuvers—we've learned that public land bordering government land is never completely safe.

ABOVE: A great horned owl fledgling in Picture Canyon.
FACING PAGE: The expanse of Picture Canyon unfolds in this spring scene.

# The Future of Colorado's Great Plains

*Our task must be to free ourselves...*
*by widening our circle of compassion*
*to embrace all living creatures*
*and the whole of nature and its beauty.*
— Albert Einstein

The will of the people has prevailed—Piñon Canyon and the Comanche National Grassland are expected to remain intact. Coloradans of both present and future generations will appreciate the land for its unique qualities that make it the soul of the Great Plains.

We are living in historic times on the Great Plains, actually making history with the rapid pace of preservation, while conservationists, land managers and land owners are speaking the same language—a language of sustainable land management. Private land owners have a bigger stake in the health of their land than at any time in plains history.

Where it is possible, The Nature Conservancy is conserving properties by leasing them to ranchers like the Tanners, who have decades of experience. Cattle grazing is managed to mimic the movement of bison to the benefit of dependent creatures. The recent Smith Ranch land purchase in Lincoln County protects 2,000 acres of wetlands, more than 200 playa lakes and nearly 50,000 acres of premier shortgrass prairie habitat. Successful prairie conservation will depend on a host of strategies, including protecting working cattle ranches, establishing preserves, keeping rivers and streams flowing, and, most of all, bringing conservationists and producers (particularly ranchers) together to explore ways to work together to achieve a shared vision for the prairie.

In addition to the landmark IBA program, Audubon Colorado and other conservation groups are working with Congress to include and strengthen well-funded incentives in the federal Farm Bill that will help grassland ranchers manage their properties for overall ecosystem health that is compatible with wildlife. The general public benefits from healthy grasslands, which provide habitats for prairie wildlife, while performing important ecosystem functions such as protecting soil, absorbing water, and acting as carbon sinks for a world increasingly threatened by excess carbon in the atmosphere.

The Buffalo Commons idea has weathered the initial ridicule and is actually happening, with Frank and Debra Popper lauded in many places for their vision and courage to start the conversation. The Buffalo Commons concept is discussed as a regional metaphor today, encouraging coexistence with wildlife while creating a sustainable prairie community. Each area has unique qualities and threats, so the metaphor takes on different meanings in different areas. Ultimately, the land will decide how best to manage its various resources.

The governor of North Dakota, Edward Schafer, was a vocal critic of Buffalo Commons when the proposal was first released. He is now among the strongest backers of the concept. Bison ranchers can now get loans at state and other banks, while receiving technical assistance from the agricultural extension service. Former cable television magnate Ted Turner is feeding his restaurant customers free-roaming bison raised on his spacious ranches, while building on his vision of developing one continuous bison ranch from Canada to Mexico. Turner's ranches encourage biodiversity and welcome all native creatures—wolves, bears and mountain lions included. On the Big Open of the northern Great Plains, the American Prairie Foundation is reaching its goal of accumulating land and providing prime habitat for the full suite of native prairie creatures, including pure bison and black-footed ferrets. The U.S. Fish and Wildlife Service has achieved its goal of releasing genetically pure bison on six refuges in an effort to further protect and diversify the gene pool. These bison will be managed as one herd, called "metapopulation management." They are also educating the public about the value of this charismatic beast on our prairies. I hope there will come a time when visitors are no longer content to see a few bison; they will wish to see a few *thousand* bison!

Rocky Mountain Arsenal and Rocky Flats National Wildlife Refuges are nearly finished with their cleanup. Rachel Carson, a 30-year employee of the U.S. Fish and Wildlife Service, and one of our most celebrated conservationist authors, would be very proud.

It has been said that re-introducing missing and extirpated species is a step backwards to the times before civilization, that we have moved beyond a wilderness prairie. Yes, we have traveled far in 150 years, but as society grows increasingly isolated from wilderness and wildlife, we crave refuge. That is why the small herd of bison at Rocky Mountain Arsenal NWR is so important and has garnered worldwide attention. We need wild places to relieve the stresses of everyday life and to reconnect with something that stirs deep in our hearts. The biggest step *forward* that our society can take is to preserve large parcels of grassland, complete with bison, prairie dogs, black-footed ferrets, beaver, elk, pronghorn, and hundreds of native prairie birds. Our proudest legacy will be to preserve such a place, where future generations can see, hear, smell and touch the wonders of the Great Plains.

# Afterword

*Nature does nothing uselessly.*
*—Aristotle*

My wife and I recently rode our mountain bikes across the Timpas unit of the Comanche National Grassland, grinning ear-to-ear as we raced steel contraptions on an endless road across the verdant plain. We had shared three days in the grassland and I proudly observed as the prairie worked its magic on Marla. Sharing a soul connection, this was just one of those perfect days, gliding carefree under a brilliant blue sky as we pedaled through an ocean of grass. The American people, not the Army, own the very road we were traveling on. I reflected on my journey to make this book and the struggles of the dreamers who settled the land—the mountains just out of reach, the blistering sun too much to bear. My time has been spent making pictures and scratching notes, trying to piece together a collage of images that make up a vision of the western Great Plains. Quite accidentally, forks in the road led me to fascinating people who have spent their entire lives on the land, people who welcomed me into their homes and shared their stories. I keep asking *The Question*, "What is it about the prairie?", still searching for the secrets of this place that enraptures people from all walks of life. We want to know and experience our Western heritage, and understand our place in this complex, harsh and fragile landscape and all of its star qualities. Whether we call ourselves conservationists or ranchers, or simply lovers of nature, our bond is the common place where our passion, hopes and dreams overlap.

May we dream big enough.

The road to Picketwire,
Comanche National Grassland.

Everywhere that I traveled on this journey, people responded enthusiastically, offering to help. This project would simply not have been possible without your support. Thank you for being so generous with your time, knowledge and sharing the land that you so passionately work to preserve every day.

Dean Rundle gave me the opportunity at Rocky Mountain Arsenal National Wildlife Refuge and the entire staff made me a part of the family. In particular, Sherry James opened many doors (and continues to), Mindy Hetrick turned me into a birder, Sherry Skipper welcomed me into the biological community, Aaron Rinker let me tag along on a lengthy deer study, Amy Thornburg shared the wonder of Rocky Flats designated NWR, and Steve Berendzen kept me on as volunteer photographer. My thanks to the refuge staff. Suzanne O'Neill of the Rocky Mountain Arsenal Wildlife Society and the Colorado Wildlife Federation has been a great friend from the beginning.

Mike Lockhart has spent more than a decade protecting black-footed ferrets and their habitat and graciously allowed me to photograph our most endangered mammal. Gary Graham not only helped shape the scope of the book, but spent many hours discussing Audubon's conservation perspective. Bill Ulfelder of The Nature Conservancy provided access to TNC lands, and introduced me to the new Shortgrass Prairie Partnership, enabling me to meet the people who are changing the face of conservation in Colorado. Frogard Ryan, William Burnidge, Chris Broda-Bahm, and Jan Koenig of TNC have been supportive as well.

Jack and Peg Emery kindly flew Marla and me over the Pawnee Buttes for a great "raptor's-eye" view of the land.

Thanks to Fran Blanchard of Plains Conservation Center, a kind and knowledgeable naturalist; John Bustos and Mike Trujillo of the U.S. Forest Service, thank you for your support; and Tom Peters, also of the U.S.F.S., who helped me understand conservation issues facing the Comanche National Grassland. Thanks as well to Mark Gershman and Lynn Riedell of Boulder Open Space and Mountain Parks.

Dave and Marlene Groves opened the door to their Buffalo Groves Ranch and shared their wonderful bison ranching lifestyle. Dick and Sandra Tanner, Carl and Sherry Stogsdill, Lucille Egli-McIntyre, her husband, Bob, and Ernie Mauer welcomed me into their homes and told their stories. Lucille shared her family pictures and I appreciate her friendship.

In the beginning, David Middleton helped create a road map to turn this dream into a reality and has been a great mentor.

Todd Caudle, Mr. Skyline Press and Colorado Mountains, took a chance by publishing a prairie book. Thanks to Todd for bringing my imagery to life with your creative vision, keeping me off balance with your great sense of humor, and for being a trusted friend.

I sincerely apologize to anyone who I may have missed. Any errors in the text are mine alone.

An old windmill stands watch over the construction of new wind turbines on the Pawnee.